THE *Love* TRIANGLE

THE Love TRIANGLE

WHAT EVERY COUPLE NEEDS FOR A SUCCESSFUL MARRIAGE

.

RENEE BEAMER

NEW YORK

THE *Love* TRIANGLE

WHAT EVERY COUPLE NEEDS FOR A SUCCESSFUL MARRIAGE

ISBN 978-1-61448-238-3 paperback
ISBN 978-1-61448-239-0 eBook
Library of Congress Control Number: 2012931612

Morgan James Publishing
The Entrepreneurial Publisher
5 Penn Plaza, 23rd Floor,
New York City, New York 10001
(212) 655-5470 office • (516) 908-4496 fax
www.MorganJamesPublishing.com

Cover Design by:
Rachel Lopez
www.r2cdesign.com

Interior Design by:
Bonnie Bushman
bonnie@caboodlegraphics.com

In an effort to support local communities, raise awareness and funds, Morgan James Publishing donates a percentage of all book sales for the life of each book to Habitat for Humanity Peninsula and Greater Williamsburg.

Get involved today, visit
www.MorganJamesBuilds.com.

To Rob and Lisa Bouldin.

TABLE OF CONTENTS

Acknowledgements

A special thanks goes to my husband, Jonathon Beamer, for giving me inspiration, vision and expertise throughout this project. I think I would have abandoned the work if you had not been that constant voice of encouragement.

Thank you, Jillian Freeland, Liesa Glander and Jennifer Villarreal for freely giving of yourselves to edit and provide feedback. Your support is greatly appreciated.

EPHESIANS 5:22- 33
(The Message)

Wives, understand and support your husbands in ways that show your support for Christ. The husband provides leadership to his wife the way Christ does to His Church, not by domineering but by cherishing. So just as the Church submits to Christ as He exercises such leadership, wives should likewise submit to their husbands.

Husbands, go all out in your love for your wives, exactly as Christ did for the Church- a love marked by giving, not getting. Christ's love makes the Church whole. His words evoke her beauty. Everything He does and says is designed to bring the best out of her, dressing her in dazzling white silk, radiant with holiness. And that is how husbands ought to love their wives. They're really doing themselves a favor- since they're already "one" in marriage.

No one abuses his own body, does he? No, he feeds and pampers it. That's how Christ treats us, the Church, since we are part of His body. And this is why a man leaves father and mother and cherishes his wife. No longer two, they become "one flesh." This is a huge mystery, and I don't pretend to understand it all. What is clearest to me is the way Christ treats the Church. And this provides a good picture of how each husband is to treat his wife, loving himself in loving her, and how each wife is to honor her husband.

INTRODUCTION

I went to the altar to marry my beloved in December 1990. Our courtship had begun four years earlier and culminated with a one-year engagement. Making a covenant with God in uniting with my husband was serious business. I wanted our marriage to be successful. Don't we all? I look back now and consider the obstacles: we were young and immature in our faith. Although we had committed to going to church on Sundays with his parents, we still had so much to learn. Pastor James Cheshier made sure that his church family learned God's design for marriage. As newlyweds, Jon and I sat under his teaching on Ephesians 5:22-33 and learned that it takes more than the love shared between two people to have a lasting marriage.

Shortly before our wedding day, my grandfather asked me if I wanted my marriage with Jon to work. He had me captive to his advice because I needed wisdom. He said that if I keep Jesus centered in my life, God will put everything else in its proper place. Knowing that my grandparents had been married for 49 years at that point, I reasoned that he spoke truth. I had already invited Jesus into my life, but now I invited Him into our marriage, and even though I did not know what it should look like or how it would be done, I decided to partner with God and build a household of faith. That was over 20 years ago. I have no regrets as I look back. My marriage is extremely blessed, and I believe that it will continue to see increase. God has taught us about this exciting Love Triangle, and I can say with confidence, "A chord of three strands is not quickly broken" (Ecclesiastes 4:12b).

Chapter One

MARRIAGE
MODELS

"To have and to hold, till death do us part" - sounds like it is for keeps, doesn't it? Do we really mean the marriage vows we state? Is there ever a time when either party is thinking in the back of the mind, "until something better comes along," or "until you hurt me badly…?"

Prince William and Kate Middleton stated their vows of marital devotion in the "Wedding of the Century," but news coverage throughout the day included speculation over the lasting quality of the couple. Is the love between the royal couple sufficient for marital bliss? Is the love we share with our beloveds the kind that lasts?

1

The wedding vows speak of an unbroken covenant, but too many fickle-hearted cannot fulfill them. Consider, however, Oscar and Mary's testimony given their 75th wedding anniversary (yes, you read it correctly)! Mary said, "When we got married, people said it was forever, and we were so young and stupid that we believed it!"

Some find the vow "till death do us part" hard to incorporate into their belief system because it's never been modeled for them. It is almost like asking a student new to Calculus to work a difficult problem without showing the steps to solve it. He asks, "How do I find the answer?" The instructor responds, "That's for you to figure out." The average student would not get very far. If making marriage work has not been modeled for you, how do you go about learning to love your spouse in good times and bad?

Many marriage models are available, but all may not be reliable. A child's upbringing is the most common marriage example. I hope that when you were growing up, your family was intact with loving parents displaying mutual love and respect at all times. Unfortunately, a variety of circumstances may prevent this from being a reality. Although my childhood was a happy one, there were definitely troubles in our home. Only now as an adult can I clearly see those problems were stemming from an absence of Christ in our hearts.

However, my love for family and home life began when I was a little girl. My mother left her career and stayed at home to raise us. My older siblings were in school, and mom and I did everything together. It was at that formative time in my life that I decided I would have the same type of lifestyle. I dreamed of growing up, getting married, having children, and taking care of a home and family.

Today, my life is fulfilled as I realize this childhood dream. I am the grown-up whom I desired to be so long ago. While I am presently in the season of childrearing, I understand from many who have gone before me that it passes quickly. Therefore, I have this strong mandate within to dedicate myself to doing it well. After all, there is only one chance. Soon, our two children will be grown and leading their adult lives they have long dreamed of. What heritage will Jon and I have passed on to them? I trust they will know that their parents love God passionately and are devoted to each another. They will confidently know that they are loved, accepted, and fully supported by us. I anticipate them seeing that though mom and dad have been together for many years, they are still just as happily married as always. This is something of utmost importance to me: I want them to see how marriage should work.

Children understand the connection between their parents' lasting marriage and their own bright futures. Maybe children cannot actually verbalize it, but they definitely relate their happiness and security to their parents' success. Sadly, just the opposite is true. Young children will blame themselves for a divorce; they assume that they are the source of their parents' unhappiness. As a teenager facing the dismantling of my home, I did not blame myself. My reasoning mind knew that my parents had unresolved issues that were unrelated to parenting me. I remember, though, my future looking very bleak. Prior to the restoration of my parents' marriage, I had stopped dreaming because I saw little hope for the days ahead.

Where do we look for marriage models today? Seeing that young people in the United States are very entertainment driven, many look to the examples of famous entertainers. I cannot help but notice the magazine covers in the checkout lines. Some stars seem to get all of the press' attention with their "flavor-of-the-week" love interest. Undoubtedly, there are headlines announcing weddings and divorces in equal numbers.

What about all of the other media influences on the belief that marriages are disposable? Infidelity is regularly presented as the expected norm, and it makes me wonder why we choose to invest one or two hours of time in entertainment when the message being imprinted on minds is to look for something better elsewhere? I really fear for the society that idolizes a blasé attitude toward the institution of marriage. The problem with these models is they normalize the sentiment that a spouse can justify divorce based on unhappiness. How many broken homes will it take before we realize the strength of our nation has been compromised?

The upcoming generation has a great opportunity to partner with God in His work of restoring families and a nation.

The upcoming generation has a great opportunity to partner with God in His work of restoring families and a nation. They can decide to be counter-culture and have a resolve like Daniel's to not be defiled by their environment.1 I charge the young married couples to build households of faith that bring glory to God. They can do this by detaching themselves from entertainment that celebrates immorality. They must lay down their idols and worship God alone. It is an absolute choice and not a combination of the two. A major influence of worldly standards with a little bit of God mixed in will prove to be a snare in marriage. Conformity to the patterns of this world is seen in the life of a couple determined to set their own course in life without any counsel from God. They go to church on Sundays and they have even served in a church project or ministry. But a relationship with Christ is missing. The working of the Spirit of God to produce spiritual fruit is absent in their hearts and home.

For each household that easily caves to the onslaught of forces set to oppose making marriage work, our strength as a nation is increasingly weakened. To prove this point, we only have to look at America's recent history. During the time of my parents' childhood, the nation was recovering from a difficult, yet victorious, involvement in World War II. The "Builders" generation consists of those born before 1945 and is characterized by men and women who got the job done. They made costly sacrifices and worked hard to successfully complete every task before them, including marriage. Divorce was not common in that era and was even considered shameful.

Within twenty years, a noticeable decay in the family unit is detected as divorces increase, drug experimentation is on the rise, and prayer is removed from schools. The departure from a sense of community and a replacement with self-reliance defined the "Boomer" generation. Many challenged conventional family-life and adapted instead a "do your own thing" motto. 2 Now, thirty years later, we encounter the statistic that 50% of marriages in America will end in divorce. 3 In fact, many who are divorcing today come from divorced parents themselves. This current trend within the "Millennial" generation throws the state of the family into a crisis as relativism spreads the belief that truth is whatever you define it to be.

We need to be alert of the dangers present in this generation. We are increasingly relating to others through the advancements in technology. The e-mail communication of the past has been replaced with video chats and texting. Old friends are finding one another and building new relationships through social networks. Although the current digital age endorses a rather impersonal display of reaching out to another, the emotional connections being formed are alarming. Many find themselves entangled in adultery, completely violating their vow to marital faithfulness.

While all of these situations are far from positive, it is simply my attempt to alert the average person and cause him or her to evaluate their present influences in life. It is not uncommon to discover that we are caught up in situations that we never imagined ourselves to be in. The beauty of this reality is that we can make some choices and see things turn around for the better. We can choose to place before us the one eternal model that never fails and never fades. It is the Love Triangle that I discovered shortly before my own wedding. But, no matter what stage of marriage you are in, the Love Triangle is the answer to any and all of your challenges.

Study Questions for Chapter One

1. Is there a model marriage that you and your spouse would want to emulate?

2. What things of your upbringing do you desire to see passed down and continued in the lives of your children and grandchildren? What traits or behaviors would you prefer not be repeated?

3. What forms of entertainment do you enjoy? What messages do they promote?

4. Do you surround yourself with positive people? In what ways do they encourage you to grow spiritually?

Chapter Two

A GLANCE BACK

A Love Triangle always implies a love affair, and it could not be any truer in this case. Jesus is inviting you to experience an intimate relationship with Him. He is foundational in marriage. God Himself is the Creator of relationship and we love because He first loved us (1 John 4:19). Or, as I like to say, we desire relationship because He first desires relationship with us.

No guidance on a fulfilling and lasting marriage is complete without instruction from God's Holy Word. "Heaven and earth will pass away, but my words will never pass away," God says (Matthew 24:35). So, if God's Word will outlast all that we see with our eyes, then it is all- surpassing when it comes to instruction on marriage! In fact, Ephesians 5:22-33 contains many treasures and a deep mystery hidden within the verses. The discovery will lead to a greater appreciation for God's marriage design as well as a thrust into the arms of the Lover of your soul.

Ephesians 5:22 introduces the marriage sermon with, "Wives, submit to your husbands as to the Lord." As I personally wonder why God chooses to first instruct the female and not the male counterpart, I go back to Genesis 3 where God deals with the sin of Adam and Eve, the first married couple. God initially confronts Adam to hear his account of their eating fruit from the forbidden tree. But when it is time to reveal the consequences of their sin, God first addresses Eve. This is not to be interpreted as Eve being the one to bear the greater weight of their sin. It is simply God's way of doling out the consequence that she will suffer before He addresses the heart of the matter: Adam had been given charge over everything in the Garden, but he failed. God gave Adam the responsibility to protect the wellbeing of all He had created, including Eve. Had Adam remained obedient, Eve would have been prevented from rebelling against the command of God. Adam was her covering, her protection and security. It is understood from Genesis 2:16-18 that Adam was the one entrusted with the command from God. He knew not to eat from the tree of the knowledge of good and evil, and we know that he conveyed the mandate to his wife because she repeated it in her conversation with the Serpent. However, Adam's failure to shepherd Eve in the truth led to their being deceived.

I do not seek to incite an Adam-bashing session with the illumination of what happened in the Garden. The Fall was bound to occur whether the first man had been Adam, Joe or Moe! God knew this when He created mankind, yet, He still chose us to walk in relationship with Him. It is a thrill to think on this most divine romance. God knew that in creating man, He would have to provide a perfect substitute for the payment of all of mankind's sin. Amazing, isn't it? The Cross of Christ was always Plan A. It is also amazing to think that Jesus was always prepared to go to the Cross in order to pay for our sin. You see, God could have chosen to walk in intimate relationship with a different species, one that does not have the freewill to rebelliously turn from Him and His ways. But God's heart desires sacred relationship in which His children *choose* to love and obey their Creator. It is romance in its purest form. "I choose you. Will you also choose Me?" Psalm 14:2 states, "The Lord looks down from heaven on the sons of men to see if there are any who understand, any who seek God." God is seeking to be sought by man whom He created. He lives up to His name, Emmanuel or "God With Us," every time that we read in His Word, "I will be with you." God does not force His relationship upon us; however, the Bible states that if we seek Him, He will be found.1 It is not unlike our own heart's desire for intimate human relationship. We want a healthy and fulfilling friendship or romantic relationship out of another's desire to be with us. Would there be any personal satisfaction in hearing a spouse say, "I only spent time with you today because I know that is what I should do." Do we really expect God to feel any differently? Would He be satisfied with the relationship hearing, "I only worship you because I am supposed to do so." No, He does not want robotic subjects in relationship with Him. He wants us to seek His companionship. Consider Psalm 63:1:

> *O God, You are my God, earnestly I seek You;*
> *my soul thirsts for You, my body longs for You,*
> *in a dry and weary land where there is no water.*

So, to get back to the reality that Adam sinned against God, it is important to understand that the

Fall from grace is not an "Adam-thing," it is a "man-thing." In creating man with a freewill, God foreknew the result and planned, at the same time, the remedy for our fallen state.

The very interesting passage of scripture found in Genesis 3:14-19 makes clear that God cannot and will not overlook sin. To the Serpent, He states, "Because you have done this [deceptive deed], cursed are you above all the ... animals." God also prophesies Satan's lot with the words, "I will put enmity between you and the woman, and between your offspring and hers; he [Jesus] will crush your head and you will strike his heel." From the beginning of man's existence on earth, God foretold the coming Messiah: the Savior and Rescuer of man and the Deliverer from the punishment of sin.

Then God states to Eve that her childbearing will involve pain and she will desire her husband's rule, but he will rule over her. Finally, to Adam, He says, "Because you listened to your wife and ate from the tree... 'Cursed is the ground because of you; through painful toil you will eat of it all the days of your life.'"

I find that the language plainly indicates whom God charges with the responsibility for the Fall of man: Satan, the Serpent, for his deception, and Adam, who abandoned his rule. To both, God pronounced punishment stating, "because you...." While He does not release Eve from the suffering of consequences, God also avoids linking her behavior with the soon to be realized painful results. It is here that we first discover the importance of the husband's covering of his wife. Remember, the covering is intended for her blessing of love and protection. But in this case, God requires Adam's covering in the form of taking on the responsibility of Eve's sin. Did Adam step up in this moment and say, "Don't blame her, God. It was all my fault?" Clearly he did not. When God first addressed Adam's sin, his quick reply utilized the infamous blame game. "The woman you put here with me- she gave me some fruit from the tree, and I ate it" (Genesis 3:12). Did you see the double portion of blame there? Not only did the woman cause him heartache, but also God Himself seemingly made the mistake of placing her with Adam. That is a loving Father to not smack him into non-existence at that point! No, Adam did not take the opportunity to be chivalrous. Instead, it is God who shows man that he will bear the responsibility for his wife: both in her successes and in her failures.

One crucial element of understanding gained from Genesis is that the curses actually illuminate the peaceful existence of man before the Fall. Only after the Fall was there enmity between the woman and the Serpent and between her offspring and his offspring, pain in childbearing, competition for rule in the home, and toil in man's labors. God's plan of obedience prior to the Fall was absent of all such strife. So, what would that have looked like if everything went according to the design for man's existence in Eden? Most importantly, Adam would have prevented the serpent from convincing Eve to doubt God's command. Adam is not mentioned at all during the exchange between the Serpent and Eve. In fact, his name appears in the text only after she had examined the fruit, had seen that it was pleasing to the eye and then tried it. The obedient overseer would have ruled over the serpent and prevented his deceptive talk from finding a receptive ear. I can remember times as a child living on a farm when my father would take a rake out to a tree near the house and coax a snake out of the tree and back into the woods. Unfortunately, it was an act that he had to repeat until the unwanted guest got the message. (In case there is confusion regarding why the snake was not killed with the rake, it is because they are essential in controlling the mice population!) That is exactly the action lacking in Eden as God had already charged Adam to "rule over the fish of the sea and the birds of the air, over the livestock, over all the earth, and over all the creatures that move along the ground" (Genesis 1:26).

Adam's rightful dominion under God's authority would have consequently led to his rightful rule as Eve's husband. Having failed God in following through on His command, he was now susceptible of failing Eve. Perhaps the power struggle in marriage began at that point. The design for a marriage built upon trust would have been easily accomplished if trustworthiness had been displayed in Eden. The woman, having known her place in creation as a suitable helper to her husband, would have gladly submitted to his word as he proved himself faithful to God. Perfect confidence in her husband's authority would have prevented Eve and all subsequent generations of wives from acting in distrust and defiance to the man's place of authority.

This is a real problem in many households in our society: women somehow stepping into the role of authority in the home and men acting in submission. I do not think it is comical to hear a man say, "I just do what the boss says." I cannot think of anything more distasteful than a weakened man seeking to fulfill every command of a dominating wife. It is more than a personal opinion that has me opposed to this picture;

it is a clear understanding of God's design for marriage as laid out in scripture. Remember, when God made known his punishment for Adam's sin, He clearly stated where Adam faltered: "Because you listened to your wife…." This is not an attempt to build false doctrine that states every wife's idea is a bad one and leads to sin! God simply corrects Adam for esteeming his wife's word above the Word of the Lord.

> *The heavenly reality that God created in the form of the Garden and its inhabitants was to be expanded until it covered the earth.*

The peaceful order that Adam and Eve experienced briefly has been rightly reinstituted in the dominion of man over the earth. Christ fulfilled the Genesis 3 prophesy by offering His life as the final sacrifice. His blood covers our sins, and they were nailed to the cross; the price has been paid! Christ was raised from the dead and lives forevermore at the right hand of the Father and intercedes for us so that we may be strengthened to carry out our regained dominion. Before Jesus left His disciples, He stated, "I confer on you a kingdom…" (Luke 22:29). As Christ was about to ascend to the

Father in heaven, He restored the rule and authority over the earth to man, specifically to those who would soon be empowered by the Holy Spirit with the resulting character of Christ to rule righteously over all that is entrusted to them.

Many Christians do not understand our God-given position of divine dominion over the earth. It is especially important for married couples to grasp this concept, because their union, along with the Spirit of Christ, creates a complete and righteous rule that enables them to fulfill the mandate of God spoken originally to Adam and Eve. Genesis 1:27-28 speaks of God creating man and woman in His own image, blessing them, and saying, "Be fruitful and increase in number; fill the earth and subdue it." The heavenly reality that God created in the form of the Garden and its inhabitants was to be expanded until it covered the earth. Consider these words from the psalmist David:

When I consider your heavens, the work of your fingers, the moon and the stars, which You have set in place, what is man that you are mindful of him, the son of man that You care for him. You made him a little lower than the heavenly beings and crowned him with glory and honor. You made

him ruler over the works of your hands; You put
everything under his feet" (Psalm 8: 3 – 6).

The mission is the same for today. When we pray the Lord's Prayer, we prove the mission true: "Your kingdom come, Your will be done on earth as it is in heaven" (Matthew 6:10). Although singles, children, and widowed are capable and successful in the mission of expanding the kingdom of God, married couples that know the above truth are very effective and needed. They understand a blessedly intimate relationship that most closely depicts the intimacy in one's relationship with God. They experience communion with one another and can more precisely convey the desired communion of the Creator with the created. Is it any wonder why marriages are under attack by the spiritual forces of evil? If you and your spouse deem to serve the Lord God with your lives, then your marriage is a threat to the kingdom of darkness. Take a look around you and notice all that Satan has introduced in our present culture to destroy the sanctity of marriage.

I pray that already you are experiencing an opening of your eyes to a new reality. The glance back to the Garden was absolutely necessary for the understanding of marriage according to God's design. We now forge ahead to the New Testament scriptures and continue to build our marriages on the eternal truth of God's Word.

Study Questions for Chapter Two

1. According to God's creation of husband and wife, what are the distinct roles of the two? What is their united mission?

2. Do you and your spouse see yourselves united for God's purpose to expand His kingdom upon the earth? What obstacles, if any, are preventing your grasp of this mission?

3. Who bears the greater weight of authority in your marriage? Are you both fulfilled in your current roles as husband and wife?

4. Do you and your spouse find it difficult to trust one another? Identify the specific areas where you are challenged and pray for understanding and strength to trust.

Chapter Three

THE
BEAUTY OF
SUBMISSION

Before we finish unearthing all the truths found in Ephesians 5:22-33, we will have looked at every angle there is to explore. For now, we will concentrate on the wife's role in marriage. Ephesians 5:22 states, "Wives, submit to your husbands as to the Lord." I think we ladies can agree not to get offended because of God's choice to first clarify the wife's responsibility in marriage. Just like we saw in Genesis, God will deliver the heavier responsibility to the one with the greater role in due time.

The wife's submission to her husband as to the Lord infers that she has a relationship with the Lord God; she knows that His intentions toward her are good (Psalm 23:6), and she receives His joy by being obedient to Him (John 15:10-11). If you have not cultivated such a relationship with God in which the above truths are part of your core beliefs, I implore you to begin today. God desires to be known and His presence enjoyed in our daily lives. To begin a relationship with Him, simply confess that you are a sinner in need of His grace (Romans 3:23-24). Believe upon the redemptive work of Jesus on the Cross, the shedding of His blood to cover your sins (Ephesians 1:7).

Some may question why blood is necessary as a cleansing agent for sin. Romans 6:23 states that the wages of sin is death. Death was initiated in the Garden when Adam and Eve sinned, became aware of their nakedness and felt shame. God's first act of atonement came through the death of one of His created animals so that He could produce skins to cover Adam and Eve. Can you imagine how difficult it was for God to slaughter one of His own creatures? As a child growing up on a farm, I experienced a great sense of loss each time an animal was butchered. But God is more than a livestock owner; He actually wove the fibers together to form the animal that He would later choose to sacrifice.

God's first and final atonement for the sins of mankind produced the same result. Through the shedding of precious blood, we are not left uncovered and riddled with shame. Instead, we are robed in Christ's righteousness that we could never earn on our own merit.

To receive salvation, we need to also believe that Jesus resurrected from the grave and is at the right hand of the Father in heaven (Romans 8:34). And, because Christ is in that position, He says that we can ask Him for anything in His Name, and He will do it (John 14:12-14). Ask God to fill you with His Holy Spirit, so that you may walk in victory as you live each day to please Him (Acts 2:4, Luke 11:13). It's important to join a community of believers where Jesus is exalted and the Word of God is instructed with application to life. When you read God's Word, ask Him to give you understanding. Pray about what you read by simply talking with God. It's an exciting adventure, Friend! If you have made that decision today, I would love to hear from you and encourage you in your newly discovered faith. For me personally, my initial desire to recommit my life to Christ was so that I would have His love and power to be able to enjoy a fulfilling and godly marriage. I find God to be abundantly faithful as He grows and strengthens my relationship with my husband and with Himself.

Bible reading plans are an excellent source for the needed discipline to daily read God's Word. There are many options worth exploring. Check out Bible applications for your phone or computer to find one that suits your interest. The following website offers my favorite reading plan: http://www.bible-reading.com.

We submit to our husbands with the understanding that God protects us in that humble state.

A wife's submission to her husband should not be a jolting concept in light of our review of Genesis chapter 3. However, if the inner voice within you ladies is demanding, "Ain't no man gonna tell me what to do," try to stay with me here! Remember that Adam was charged with the care of everything in the Garden and was God's provision for Eve's protection. Therefore, we submit to our husbands with the understanding that

God protects us in that humble state. There is purity and peace in this submission that was always inherent in God's plan for marriage. The fact that Eve stepped out of that protection (again, Adam should have been watchful) is the reason that God must now instruct us to submit. God's beautiful design is accessible to us all now that man's dominion on the earth has been restored through the victorious work of Christ. However, Satan still has access to our minds! He deceives us, as he did Eve, causing us to doubt God's Word. Doubt may appear non-threatening, but when we understand how easily it leads to deception, we will be careful to avoid its rebellious fruit. Eve disobeyed God because she believed the lie.

It is time to be women who feed on the Word of God. In doing so, we will not be swayed to doubt what is plainly presented as truth. We can trust that God means what He says. Maybe it is worth reading again: "Wives submit to your husbands as to the Lord." Simple. Truly it is easy when looking at the parallel between our submission to our spouse and to the Lord. Remember, the Lord plans good and not harm for us all the days of our lives (Jeremiah 29:11). Who wouldn't want to submit to that style of care? The Lord provides for all of our needs and even knows them in advance of us (Philippians 4:19, Matthew 6:8). Sign me up for the never-lacking state of relationship! God's provision, found in these examples and others, is in direct correlation with our submission. The scripture implies that as we expect this type of care from the Lord, we can expect it from our husbands as well.

Consider, however, why a wife's submission to her husband is an anomaly. In the work place, submission is common practice. My boss says that he will set rules for me to abide by, and if I choose to cooperate with the standards required by my job description, he will reward my obedience with pay and job security. The boss rules; I submit. Perhaps we can glean the same understanding from the teacher/student relationship. The teacher has a syllabus of work to be accomplished by the student during the designated time that they are in a working relationship. The teacher's standard of classroom behavior and student responsibilities are made known so that the student can rise to the level of expectation in his learning the material, complete all work and receive a promotion in the form of a passable grade. The teacher rules, the student submits. Coming under the authority of another is not at all a foreign concept; however, rebellion to God's established authority in marriage is commonly present in our homes.

I believe that as a consequence of the Fall, women will naturally vie for the husband's headship. When God made known the suffering in the form of desire for her husband that would come upon Eve, He used the Hebrew word *tesuqah,* meaning strong desire. This is the same word used in Genesis 4:7 when God tells Cain, "… sin is crouching at your door; it *desires* to have you, but you must master it."3 This type of desire is indeed not romantic. It is lustful because the motive is to overcome another's rightful position. Ephesians 5:23 states, "For the husband is the head of the wife as Christ is the head of the Church, His body, of which He is the Savior." God has settled the matter and clearly established the husband as the head.

Let's look at God's directive for the wife as lived out by a young couple seeking to honor His plan for marriage. The two will make a wealth of financial decisions including where to live and raise a family. The decision-making process does not eliminate the submissive wife from offering wisdom and guidance, but ultimately, the decision comes down to the husband's determination of what is best for her protection. While the wife's input on a larger and newer home in a desirable community is also appealing to her husband, he carefully weighs his responsibility for the care of his family and opts instead for a less expensive home that they could still afford if one of them should lose their job. As it turns out, the wife decides she would like to stay home from work just a few years later upon the glorious discovery that they are expecting their first child. Because she did not make the mistake of demanding or manipulating her desire for the more expensive home, she is now free to enjoy the experience of raising children without the hardship that results from being torn between family and career.

Many wives like myself can attest to the above scenario being a reality. Earlier in our marriage, I really wanted to live in one of the new homes built and owned by Jon's family in a subdivision that they developed in Williamsburg, Virginia. At one time, there were 8 recently constructed houses for sale, and I reasoned that surely the owner's son could get a drastic discount. Touring an expansive kitchen one day, I asked myself if I really wanted the dream to become a reality. I quickly assessed that we would be mortgaged to the hilt and that I would never know my ultimate luxury of being a stay-at-home mom.

The real test of submission came a few years later. At that time, Jon was beginning a career in the custom home building business and purchased a lot for us to build upon in that same neighborhood. I was ecstatic to see my wish come true. There were so many positive reasons for us to make that move. Our children were growing and needed a safe outdoor space to play, and this lot had a big yard and an acre of woods to explore. Jon's travel time to work each day would be eliminated. Also, we budgeted well so that we could afford the mortgage on his salary. Yet, throughout the building process, he was reserved and not showing the same level of excitement that I had. As the months passed, he appeared increasingly uneasy with the thought of relocating. I assumed that he was uncomfortable with the idea of moving away from the only city that he had known as home. It was not a move of great distance by any means, but some people simply cannot handle change. However, that was not the case. Jon lacked peace in his spirit, and when he asked God to clarify, he knew that we were not supposed to move into our home that was nearly finished. He now shares that he dreaded the moment he had to tell me.

I remember the day well. It was December 7, and I drove up to check on the house after my morning Bible study class ended. Some finishing touches had been done in the kitchen and baths, and I wanted to inspect the progress. I entered the foyer and started up the stairwell. I remember looking around as I climbed the stairs and sensing a voice saying, "This is not your house." I quickly dismissed the "thought," because I knew very well that this was my house. I had already moved in mentally and knew where every piece of furniture was going to be placed in a matter of weeks. Before I left the house to head back home, Jon said that we were going to have to talk later that afternoon.

When he came home, we sat on our sofa with our Bibles on our laps while Jon shared his heart about being confident that God had shut the door on our plan to move to Williamsburg. He said that he didn't know where we were going to live, but it clearly was not going to be there. Honestly, my heart broke. I had never cried so hard. We prayed together in that moment, and as the tears soaked my open Bible, I quietly asked the Lord if there was any way the decision could be changed. My sweet Heavenly Father simply replied, "Grieve, and let go."

Hearing "no" from my husband was difficult, but hearing "no" from God was easier. I trusted Him. He says, "No" with wisdom and understanding of what lies ahead. Through this I have now learned to trust my husband because he obviously is hearing from God and desires to obey Him. This is God's plan for marriage! The husband bears the responsibility for the protection and provision of his family according to the Holy Spirit's leading.

Perhaps some of you think that it was easy for me to submit because my husband was seeking to honor God, but you cannot say the same for your spouse. Still, God's Word states that we are to submit to our husbands. If it is your desire to have godly headship over your home, gently and in love express that desire to your husband. Allow him to respond to God's leading. It was not easy for me either, but God gave us a test where He proved Himself and my husband faithful.

I have no regrets as I look back on the decision made many years ago. In fact, shortly afterwards I felt very silly about crying a single tear over a house. But God knew that there was a needed time of grief for the death of a dream. He also knew that His greater "yes" was going to thrill my heart with more than I had ever expected or imagined. That is not to say that the material blessing is the big win in this situation. The gains we experienced in following God's leading have more to do with relational, emotional and spiritual benefits. I can sum it all up by saying that the Lord spared us a ton of heartache, and for that, I am eternally grateful.

Others in our lives are eternally grateful as well. God used this test of obedience to speak loudly the call to faithfulness. So many friends and loved ones marveled at our willingness to lay down a dream. It opened the door for us to share faith in Christ, and we believe many seeds were planted. Amazing, isn't it? One physical door slammed shut opened many spiritual doors of the heart.

I share this testimony in length because I know that it strikes a chord with women. We want to make a home; it is within our genetic design. The whole notion of not moving into the custom-built home was downright offensive to a few that I talked to. I can still hear one saying, "If my husband did that to me…." But I chose not to receive that influence into my heart. I knew that the Lord intended good in His leading us elsewhere. Jon was not acting maliciously in taking something precious away from me. He was in need of God's peace above my contentment. That which was temporarily painful for him soon became the source of great joy, provision and peace for the entire family.

There have been numerous times that I have laid down my desires (often worldly and selfish), only to soon discover that I am in a greater position for God's lavish blessings because I respected my husband's authority in the home. He really is the one in place to carry the great responsibility for the now and the future of his family.

It is important to understand that a wife's struggle in marriage does not result from submission, but rather attempting to rule. The greatest hindrance to experiencing the beauty of submission is the fear of being subject to another's rule. First of all, the husband who seeks to honor God's design for marriage will not use his headship for ungodly gain. However, if the husband is not in relationship with the Father, God still asks the wife to submit to his headship for the ultimate outcome to occur. "Wives, in the same way be submissive to your husbands so that, if any of them do not believe the Word, they may be won over without words by the behavior of their wives, when they see the purity and reverence of your lives" (1 Peter 3:1-2). This instruction carries such hope for the woman who loves the Lord and desperately desires her unbelieving husband to have that same loving and trusting relationship with the Father in Heaven. It is the hope of salvation and the hope of a household united in faith. God has enabled me to witness the miraculous transformation of hearts and homes, and I encourage all believing women to continue to pray and believe for the unbelieving husbands.

The above reference to a wife's submission also enhances our understanding of the woman's power of influence. Here we see her "gentle and quiet spirit" being the very agent that leads her husband to the Lord (1 Peter 3:4), but so often we see examples of her persuasive ways being used negatively. Think of her stroking her husband's ego simply to convince him to see things her way. It is manipulation at its finest. Perhaps she is more of a nag who will complain, whine and even cry her way into getting selfish desires met. Proverbs 21:9 paints a picture of such a woman: "Better to live on a corner of the roof than share a house with a quarrelsome wife." It is plain to see here the demonic scheme of division in the home, a direct contrast to the intended plan of God to unite the husband and wife for divine authority and reign.

We will not place a great amount of focus on the negative influence of a wife simply because if we look at the truth of her positive influence in the home, we will desire it and choose to abandon all workings of a perverted nature. However, I cannot stress enough that women need to be very aware of their power of influence. Consider Eve giving the fruit to Adam so that he, too, could eat. Previously, he had received direct instruction concerning the forbidden fruit. But in Adam's desire to please her, he ate. Wives, know that your husband desires to please you, but you must not abuse it. We all can honestly attest to times that we manipulated a desired response. Can we deem not to repeat that devious scheme? Can we instead choose to trust that our husbands are leading our families in wisdom supplied from our Heavenly Father? Can we trust God to promote goodness through our men?

Let's purpose to be wives of noble character described in Proverbs 31.

> *She is worth far more than rubies.*
> *Her husband has full confidence in her*
> *and lacks nothing of value.*
> *She brings him good, not harm,*
> *all the days of her life.*

This chapter of scripture has been known to exasperate some and fascinate others. It describes in detail a wife's care of her home and family. Interestingly, right in the middle of two statements concerning her provision of bed linens and clothing, we read, "Her husband is respected at the city gate, where he takes his seat among the elders of the land" (verse 23). I find this strange. God itemizes all the ways that the wife "watches over the affairs of her household," but before finishing, He adds this statement about the favor upon her husband. I am led to believe that as wives fulfill their call to provide for their families and homes, husbands are blessed and able to fulfill their role as leaders not only in the home, but also in the community. Now that is a man of influence!

I do not believe that Scripture advocates a woman's work to only take place in the home. This passage shows that she is involved in commerce and makes purchases from her earnings that will further her ability to provide for the needs of her family and of the poor. Every married couple must assess if the wife's work outside of the home is creating neglect of matters within the home. This can be a difficult decision process. Many wives like myself have come to the conclusion that we cannot do everything. Something will undoubtedly suffer. Personally, I did not want to compromise my family for career. My husband was concerned for the loss of income since we seemed to spend everything we earned. But with some sacrifices and a huge leap of faith, we stepped out of the boat of dual incomes. Did God ever prove Himself faithful to His Word and our desires! Because we demonstrate a living and active faith in which we believe God alone is our Provider, we are positioned for His favor. Financial blessings that we experience would not have come to us if we had decided to work out our finances according to our own understanding and abilities. In the first month of my not receiving a paycheck, we won an all-expense paid trip to a tropical destination. We enjoyed several days spent at a luxurious resort that we would not have been able to afford even if I had continued to work. It was a gift from the Lord in which He quickly displayed His favor on our decision.

The submissive wife is full of trust and fully convinced that God is her Provider. In fact, her confidence is so complete that "she can laugh at the days to come" (Proverbs 31:25). She goes about her work eagerly and finds her children and husband praising her and proclaiming she is blessed. This is the way it should be as confirmed in 1Peter 3:6 where God charges wives to "do what is right and do not give way to fear." Based on God's character displayed in His divine care for each child of His, the wife can live in submission to her husband without fear or intimidation. She knows that she can trust God's design for marriage and can relinquish her autonomy for the sake of better provision and protection under His sovereignty. 1 John 4:18 states, "There is no fear in love. But perfect love drives out fear, because fear has to do with punishment." Ladies, we have nothing to fear. God has set authority over our lives, not to strip us of our desires, but instead to fill us to overflowing with love, security, positive influence, and peace. It is the beauty of submission, and it is ours to enjoy.

Study Questions for Chapter Three

1. Why is a relationship with Jesus Christ foundational to having a successful marital relationship?

2. Do you, as a wife, recognize submission to your husband as submission to the Lord (Eph. 5:22)? What benefits come down from the Father through your husband in your humble state of submission?

3. Why do you think a wife's submission to her husband is so uncommon?

4. Has God delivered a difficult "No" to you through your husband? How did you respond?

5. How does it make you feel as a wife to know that your husband needs peace with God above your contentment? Are you in favor of him making tough decisions based on that need?

6. Is there a lack of peace in any area of your family life? Would a total surrender to God's design for marriage, meaning, the husband as the head, promote peace in those areas?

7. Upon what belief or evidence have you chosen a single or dual income for your family? How long has it been since you have weighed all of the pros and cons of that decision?

8. Revisit a personal testimony resulting from a time of financial dependence upon God. Know that He wants our daily lives to be a testimony of reliance upon His supernatural provision (Matthew 5:25-34).

9. Do you, like the Proverbs 31 woman, "laugh at the days to come?" Why or why not?

10. How do you define the Beauty of Submission?

KATHY O'SULLIVAN'S STORY

I have been in love with Jesus my entire life. In fact, I cannot recall a time when I did not feel His presence or recognize His hand upon my life. Even during those periods of bad choices, bad attitudes and self-destructive behaviors (read: teenage years), I knew He was with me. His gentle voice has been such a constant source of security and strength. The older I get, the more I realize how amazingly blessed I am to have had this unadulterated closeness to my King. It is a closely guarded treasure; one I cling to and hold tightly in my heart. What a gift... what an incredible gift.

"There is such a sweet relief in letting Him lead."

I never could have imagined that anything (neither height nor depth nor principality) could shake that bond or cause me to question His faithfulness. As far as I was concerned, I was committed 100%. He, who had given His life for me, had permission to run my show. I did not want to be in control. There is such a sweet relief in letting Him lead. And it showed… He gave me an incredible husband, three beautiful and healthy children, a home and ministry opportunities galore. Life was sweet and could not get any better.

And then He asked us to enter full time ministry… "The LORD had said to Abram, 'Go from your country, your people and your father's household to the land I will show you…and I will bless you…'" (Genesis 12:1-3). We were blown away by His plans for us. We prayed steadfastly for guidance, and He provided directions one step at a time. As we faithfully obeyed each step, he faithfully set another step before us. He provided everything we needed to accomplish each task. We felt as though we were living a dream. While my husband Tim was working on resumes and setting up interviews, I was working on preparing our home for its eventual sale. We attended many interviews together, most of them in other states. We marveled at how we were growing closer than we had ever imagined possible, both to each other and to our King. The process was amazing- full of peace and joy. We received incredible support from friends and family members in the form of encouragement and prayers. Always faithful, the Holy Spirit offered us discernment over comments or counsel that were not from the throne of God. Honestly, it was like entering a time of euphoria. We were giddy with the joy of the Lord. And then He made His plan clear: "Move to Indiana… take the job at Hope Missionary Church… this is My plan for you."

We couldn't put a FOR SALE sign in our yard fast enough. Tim accepted the job, and plans were set in motion for our move. Things seemed to happen at warp speed after that. There was a contract on our house within 24 hours. Our children were excited, and we felt that overwhelming peace and joy that had followed us from the very beginning.

Then the attacks began. Soon after Tim accepted the job, we began to experience attacks from the enemy. I was in the backyard with a realtor when the neighbor's pit bull attacked me, causing significant damage to my right hand. A neighborhood conflict ensued as a result, and the police were called in at one point to handle threats made by the dog's owners. The first contract on our house fell through, leaving us with concerns over the contract of sale we had on a house in Indiana. It seemed as though things were falling apart. We stood fast in prayer, but I felt doubt and fear pouring in through every possible crack and portal.

And then I thought about my parents... I wondered how badly I was going to miss them and how badly my children would miss them. Living only eight miles down the road from my childhood home had afforded us the luxury of spending untold amounts of time with them. I counted on time with my precious mother who is such an amazing source of godly counsel in my life. How could He take us away from them? How was it fair to my children to have to live so far away from grandparents who adored them so? How were my children (two of them in middle school) going to handle the social adjustments involved with being the new kids? What about my friends? Would they forget about me? How on earth would I handle an emergency in an area where I had no family? Eight hundred miles is significantly different than eight. I was not only worried; I was suddenly terrified.

For several weeks we endured additional attacks-some minor, some a bit more tedious than others. Still, we forged ahead. Tim was a rock through the process, and I was hesitant to share my sudden feelings of dread and apprehension. I did not clearly understand them, and at the time I did not recognize them for what they were: additional attack strategies of the evil one. I was tormented for weeks by messages of fear and abandonment. I began to question just how much faith I really had. I was full of guilt over all of it. I was upset for being upset! I felt out of control.

And then it dawned on me- I felt out of control. I was out of control of everything. I had never been pressed beyond comfort because my life had been easy, and I planned well for everything. Me, I, myself… my plans, my desires, my marriage, my parents, my kids, my friends, my life… and lots of unknowns could all be summarized with one word: flesh.

I was standing at the bus stop waiting for my sweet Caleb to arrive home from a busy morning at Kindergarten when I realized what was going on. I had never been pushed out of my comfort zone, at least not far enough to feel completely vulnerable and helpless. And yet here I was- completely out of control. I realized that is exactly where God wants me to be. How had I been so selfish? How had I been so foolish? I had (have) no control. I do not want control. That is always easier said, but I was suddenly filled with an overwhelming need to dump the desire to control and just lay it all out at His feet. I was crying by then, weeping really, and I heard Him whisper, "My love, just trust Me…"

I nodded my head….

"Trust Me; I know the plans I have for you…"

I was wailing at this point and continued nodding my head up and down.

"Trust me."

The gentleness of His voice touches my heart in a way not other sound ever could. I could not have held the words in even if my mouth had been taped shut! "I trust You! I trust You! I trust You! I trust You! I trust You! I trust You!" I did not realize I was shouting until the neighbor opened his door to see what was going on. Undaunted, I kept at it. "I trust You! I trust You! I trust You!" It went on for what seemed like forever; it was pure ecstasy.

In that moment, as the yellow school bus was pulling up to the curb and my darling little 6-year old gift from God came bounding down the steps into my arms, I was filled with that peace that passes all understanding. I no longer worried about what was ahead of me. My life belongs to Him, and He is in control.

> *Trust in the Lord and do good; so you will live in the land, and enjoy security. Take delight in the Lord and He will give you the desires of your heart. Commit your way to the Lord and trust in Him, and He will do this: He will make your righteousness shine like the dawn, the justice of your cause like the noonday sun. Be still before the Lord, and wait patiently for Him. Psalm 37:3-7a*

SACRIFICIAL
LOVE

I f you grew up in a family of multiple children, you probably remember times when all were disciplined, and while you were the targeted one receiving correction, you just kept waiting for the attention to shift to someone else. We ladies can draw a parallel from that sentiment in finding ourselves ready to come out from the inspection of our role as wives in marriage and now give full attention to the husband's responsibilities.

God emphatically declares in His Word that the husband is the head of the home, and we must understand that his position comes with great cost. To whom much is given, much is expected.

53

"Husbands, love your wives, just as Christ loved the Church and gave Himself up for her to make her holy, cleansing her by the washing with water through the word, and to present her to Himself as a radiant Church, without stain or wrinkle or any other blemish, but holy and blameless. (Ephesians 5: 25-27).

God details the restorative work of Christ in the scripture above for the express purpose that husbands will completely understand their role. It should be a sobering thought for a man to take a woman as his wife, for marriage is a call to self-sacrifice. Jon learned about laying down his life even in the proposal of marriage. He worked a seasonal job to generate funds for an engagement ring knowing all the while that he could purchase a vehicle with that same sum of money. All the men nod their heads and say, "I know your pain, brother!" And those who have been married for any amount of time can add, "It is only the beginning!" Do not miss the symbolism of the wedding ceremony taking place at the altar. Something is about to be sacrificed. Only real men should await the beautiful bride's arrival, because as we are about to find out, it is going to take great strength to go the distance that a husband must travel.

Who can daily die to self and choose instead to exalt the needs of another above their own personal desires? Philippians 2:5- 8 describes Jesus' divine love by which He laid down His life for humanity:

Your attitude should be the same as that of Christ Jesus: Who, being in very nature God, did not consider equality with God something to be grasped, but made Himself nothing, taking the very nature of a servant, being made in human likeness. And being found in appearance as a man, He humbled Himself and became obedient to death-even death on a cross!

God directs husbands to live a married life with the same self-sacrificing and demonstrated love as Christ.

God directs husbands to live a married life with the same self-sacrificing and demonstrated love as Christ. We must understand that the love of Christ is divine yet produced in us through the working of the Holy Spirit.

The self-sacrificing love that God instructs the husband to demonstrate is only made possible through God's provision.

For the purpose of knowing more fully the challenge presented to husbands in loving their wives as Christ loved the Church, we must examine the battle of wills. It is not a "his will versus her will" problem, but God's will versus the husband's. Let us again go to a garden, but this time we will study the scene in Gethsemane where Christ engages in a battle of the wills. Luke, the author of one of the four gospels, describes in vivid detail Christ's suffering as He prepared to lay down His life. "And being in anguish, He prayed more earnestly, and His sweat was like drops of blood falling to the ground" (Luke 22:44). Jesus endured immeasurable stress due to the foresight of His ultimate sacrifice. He asked His Father in Heaven if there was any other way for the payment of mankind's sin to be satisfied. Nonetheless, Jesus relented and said, "…yet not my will, but Yours be done" (John 22:42).

Husbands, the call to continually sacrifice is a most difficult test. Loving your wife as Christ loved the Church may bring times of great inner turmoil. Christ understands the weakness you have experienced when tempted to not press ahead through a struggle, for He Himself was tempted in every way. Yet, He was without sin (Hebrews 4:15). When Jesus arose from His time of prayer that night, His mind was made up. He moved forward with a resolve to not turn back. It was not an easy road ahead; in fact, it was a road of intense pain. But the Lord had given His "yes" to the Father. And you, man of God, also gave Him your "yes" when you vowed to love, honor and protect your wife. There is no turning back. Just because there are difficult times does not mean that you somehow veered from the right path and selected the wrong spouse. Allow the trials to accomplish their work of refining you and your wife.

It is so important for husbands to know that they are to be intentional in the increasing sanctification of their wives. To clarify, husbands, your wives should be more holy this year than they were last year because of your influence in their lives. This gives me such great concern for men, because the majority of them do not know that they are held to account and will answer for their attitudes and behaviors when they stand before the Judge on that day. I can hear the Father ask, "What did you do to promote the holiness of the woman that you took in covenant before me with the vow to love, honor and protect?" I pray that this brings enlightenment to husbands. They are called to such a high role in the spiritual formation of their beloveds. It is not an impossible task; it's simply one that requires consistent vigilance. Husbands cannot ever lay down the responsibility; therefore, God recognizes the man as the stronger of the two.1

Ladies, do not allow this truth to upset you. It does not mean that your husband is in place to outwit or outmuscle you. It only means that his call from God to love his wife is terrifically challenging. Repeatedly, God says to our men, "love as Christ." Honestly, without Christ's reign in his life, a husband cannot perfectly fulfill his unceasing and self-sacrificing role in marriage.

> *The husband bears the authority by*
> *God to ensure that only those things*
> *beneficial to his wife's purity will*
> *come into contact with her.*

According to God's command for the husband to love his wife as Christ loved the Church, he is to do the necessary washing of his wife to make her holy. While your average man is thinking "sponge bath," the reality is a wife without "stain or wrinkle or any other blemish, but holy and blameless" (Ephesians 5:27). With so much available in this world to contaminate our minds, bodies and spirits, we can see why the cleansing is necessary. The husband bears the authority by God to ensure that only those things beneficial to his wife's purity will come into contact with her. This truth will affect what he chooses to store up in his own heart, as those things will eventually surface through his words, attitudes and behaviors. It will also cause husbands to determine carefully the church they will attend, the friends they will associate with, as well as the music, reading and other forms of entertainment they will enjoy. If a movie date with your wife includes a film replete with evil themes, the message will obviously invade her heart and compromise her purity. Proverbs 4:23 states, "Above all else, guard your heart because it is the wellspring of life." Husbands, protect your wives. Do not allow her to fall prey to deception by your decision to be relaxed with her care. The exercise of your authority in the home will determine what returns to you: a wife tainted by the world or one sanctified from its ungodly influences.

My husband surrounds himself with teachings from God's Word. It is not uncommon for me to walk into a room where the television is turned to a Christian network and I soon find myself captivated by the powerful truths presented in Scripture. So even though Jon is not directly teaching me at all times, he is seeing to the increasing sanctification through "the washing with water through the Word."

I am impressed to clarify that sanctification is not going to happen accidentally. Separating oneself from sin and being set apart to serve God only occurs in the lives of those who are intentional. This stands as a warning to husbands. As God entrusts you with your wife's total care, you cannot merely hope that she gets all she needs spiritually under your headship. You need to *know* that she is growing spiritually as you fervently present her with opportunities to mature in her faith. If it sounds like a dire mission, you understand correctly. Lay down your guard momentarily, and she is off checking out the alluring fruit and getting an earful of lies. Do you really want to put forth mediocre effort in fulfilling this mandate from God? It is your call. However, we know what happens if the man tries to blame his wife's rebellion on her own foolishness… God will deal with him. After all, the husband is the head of the wife, and he bears the responsibility to cover her.

We are not done husbands. Your greater role in marriage comes with additional instruction. Wives, this is why we should be happy to do our part of respecting our spouses in submission. As if being told to die to self is not enough, husbands are also informed that they must love their wives as their own bodies (Eph. 5:28). The assumption is that just as a man is not going to deny his appetite, he is going to give that same thorough attention and care to his wife.

I'm thinking of the old adage, "The way to a man's heart is through his stomach." It is no secret that men love their food. My father was a meat and potatoes man, and my mom worked hard to please him with her supper preparations. We all know that a man's appetite is a driving force to be reckoned with. My family enjoys watching a television show based on that theme alone. The show's host travels the nation trying out the food challenges at different eateries. Surprisingly, he almost always wins.

Let's face it: every man who loves Jesus finds his stomach coming in at a close second in regards to his devotion! That may be an exaggeration, but I only know of one man who didn't have a food passion. Our friend, Derrick, was a man of many passions, but food was not one of them. His wife was amazed at the times she was required to remind him to eat.

Your average man only needs to hear that small rumble and then runs to the refrigerator. "After all, no one ever hated his own body, but he feeds and cares for it, just as Christ does the Church- for we are members of His body" (Eph. 5:29-30). Therefore, as a husband understands his goal to keep his stomach satisfied, he is to apply the same level of attention to his wife. He will nurture her with a focused goal to please her, because "he who loves his wife loves himself" (Eph. 5:28).

As with any truth presented in God's Word, a slight twisting of the meaning could translate it into something totally different. In this case, a perverted sense of entitlement or greed would cause a wife to expect any and every desire to be met. She reasons that she should have her wish granted because her husband is to love her as much as he loves his body. But just like the body wants ten chocolate chip cookies, a wise man stops at two because he knows ten would be excessive and detrimental if that eating pattern was to continue. Because he loves his body, he makes decisions to keep it healthy.

There is such a thing as creating a monster. Buying every requested gift, doing every demanded project, taking every expected trip is to honestly teach that there is never a need for restraint. Husbands, do not answer to every whim of your wife without first weighing all matters carefully before the Lord. Understand that even though you desire to please her, sometimes, genuine love is seen in the "no." Do not reason that her tears, anger or silent treatment is not worth following your conviction. Already that mindset indicates that you are willing to lay down your headship in the marriage. If this is currently your status (second-in-command), but you and your wife want to honor the Lord God with your lives, it is your responsibility to present her with the truth and your desire to follow it.

I am a woman conveying this message to men. Women who love the Lord long for their husbands to rise to the call of being the leaders in their homes. Some may find me unreasonable in this pursuit, but I am fully convinced that change will come to our nation when the men take back their rightful place of headship in the home. I wish I could blame the breakdown of the American family on those choosing to live in rebellion, but I know the change must begin within the Church.

I fear an increased occurrence of flip-flopped marriages, especially among those of our younger generation. Due to our passion to be entertained, we are constantly presented with female- dominated households. Whether we view a feature film, a major network program or even a children's show, we laugh at the dumb dad and the "I mean business" mom who must always put him in his place. Is this just harmless comedy? Or, is it a scheme to desensitize us so that we accept the wife-in-command role as normal? It especially concerns me because our young children watch these shows repeatedly while absorbing the message mindlessly. At the same time, God's people are beginning to speak out about the inaccuracy portrayed and are calling forth men through messages in print, music and film. My advice to His children is to listen to what the Spirit is saying because it is time to rectify the damage by first ensuring proper order within our own homes.

The husband's work of self-sacrificing love and sanctification culminates in the realization of a radiant bride. Just as Christ presents to Himself "a radiant Church, without stain or wrinkle or any other blemish, but holy and blameless," the godly husband pursues the same goal for his wife. Concerning her radiance, the husband needs to assure his wife of the beauty with which he beholds her. More importantly, he assures her that the adoring gaze of her Father in Heaven is upon her. Additionally, the husband cultivates her inner beauty through the nurturing of her spirit. 1 Peter 3:3-4 states, "Your beauty should not come from outward adornment… Instead, it should be that of your inner self, the unfading beauty of a gentle and quiet spirit…." As a husband increases the opportunity for his wife to grow in her relationship with the Lord, she grows more beautiful from the inside. She continually offers her heart to the Lord, and He speaks assuredly of His love and devotion to her. When she needs to know if she is lovely, the Father replies, "How beautiful you are, my darling! Oh, how beautiful!" (Song of Songs 1:15).

Husbands, you have a role model to follow in marriage. Christ laid down His life for His Church, and you are to do the same for your wives. If the concept is going to take some time to become established in your daily attitudes and behaviors, then in the meantime, just make sure you are attending to your wife's needs as readily as you attend to those of your stomach! Feed her that which will promote her inward beauty. Clothe her in dignity. Cherish her as the prize that she truly is. When you do all of these things, goodness will come back to you. The result will be a man respected in his home.

Study Questions for Chapter Four

1. What enables a husband to love his wife as Christ loved the Church?

2. Have you, as the husband, experienced a battle of the wills when confronted by God to do the right thing concerning your family? What was the outcome?

3. In what ways are you intentional in the increasing sanctification of your wife?

4. The world is loud with messages that can take us away from the heart of God. In what areas specifically is your wife vulnerable to its tainting?

5. Do you find it difficult to follow your conviction when your wife challenges your stand? What happens if she doesn't "get her way?"

6. In what ways does your wife benefit from your covering or protection of her?

7. Do you receive the proper respect as the head of your household? If not, what changes can you make to ensure that you do have your wife's respect?

8. Sacrificial love is the beginning of the marriage covenant. How would you explain that statement to a young man planning to get married?

Jeff and Bonnie

Jeff loves his country. As a major in the United States Army, protecting our freedom is his daily business. Greater than love of country is Jeff's supreme love for his family. He and his wife, Bonnie, have been married 25 years and have four beautiful children. The couple opened their home and hearts to share with Jon and me some wonderful insights they have learned along the way.

When given an opportunity to speak into the lives of young enlisted men, Jeff counsels them to place family above career. Jeff also shares with them the importance of considering their wives' needs above their own and to never stop dating.

We can all stand to gain from Jeff's understanding of what it means for husbands to love as Christ. Jon and I were greatly impressed by this man, yet he does not pretend to have it all together. Like all of us, he is a work in progress, but what Jeff exposes will increasingly change lives for the better.

There were some incredible moments of laughter during Jeff and Bonnie's sharing. For instance, he recalls the sobriety of spirit that hit him on their wedding day. As soon as he said, "I do" and they were announced husband and wife, he took a seat! Only one explanation stands: Jeff realized the seriousness of his stated covenant, and he went into utter shock. Bonnie immediately stepped into her newly acquired role as helpmate and was able to finally coax him to get up and sign the marriage certificate.

A little bit of comic relief is needed before we get into the depth of the heart of a man. He is a man because he is the hero; he will come through every time. Jeff has portrayed godly character as a husband consistently over the years. On one specific military unit outing when all the other men went into a scandalous nightclub, Jeff remained outside the premises. He did not just wait by the door of the business, he stayed on the bus and in the dark for hours. Character like this gives him the rank of "filet mignon" in his wife's eyes. He is her choicest cut and prize. Allow Bonnie's words to sink deeply into your being as she expresses admiration for her man:

God has tried to tell me for 45 years about who He is, but man has said the wrong things about who God is. However, Jeff is the physical demonstration of Christ. He continually reinforces who I am in Christ. He repeatedly shows me Christ's love and sacrifice. I'm finally beginning to see God's love for me because I'm beginning to understand the love Jeff has for me. God has shown me that Jeff will never leave me; therefore, I know that God will never leave me nor forsake me.

When I asked Jeff why he believes Bonnie would not go looking for love from any source other than her God and her husband, she quickly jumps in to answer that she would not choose to eat dog food! I think he likes being considered her filet mignon. And he proves himself as her finest match in that he completely understands his role as a husband. Jeff prays for his wife. Daily he covers her in prayer before he leaves for work. At church, he covers her in her times of prayer. He states that in those moments he knows that she is not to be alone. If the Spirit of God leads him to speak something to her as she is pouring out her heart to the Father, he then does so. Jeff vigilantly covers Bonnie in prayer, through his own spoken blessings and through his physical presence.

> *"When it comes time for Bonnie to stand before the Father, I want her to know who she is. This is my greatest pursuit."*

Jeff also shared about a time that he increased his role in the sanctification of his wife. He implemented a study of God's Word on the topic of spiritual warfare based on his personal understanding of military war tactics. He came to the conclusion that he had been repeatedly baited by Satan to fight with his wife, and he was not going to continue to fall for it. The result? The whole family went through the lessons written and taught by dad to become better equipped to fight Satan with weapons that have divine power to "demolish arguments and every pretension that sets itself up against the knowledge of God" (2 Cor. 10:5).

Knowing how to victoriously fight a formidable foe is one matter, but Jeff's essence as a husband is for his wife to know her identity in Christ. He says, "When it comes time for Bonnie to stand before the Father, I want her to know who she is. This is my greatest pursuit."

> *Husbands, love your wives, just as Christ loved the Church and gave Himself up for her to make her holy, cleansing her by the washing with water through the word, and to present her to Himself as a radiant church, without stain or wrinkle or any other blemish, but holy and blameless (Eph. 5: 25 – 27).*

Chapter Five

JESUS,
THE ONE
WHO BONDS
THE TWO

I have eagerly anticipated writing this chapter. I almost inserted it earlier out of sheer excitement. Reason kicked in, and I decided to follow the flow of subjects presented in Ephesians 5:22-33. First we explored the role of the wife, then that of the husband, and now the mystery of Christ. I have asked God to change this mystery into a Love Triangle revelation!

Notice the original relationship involving three noted in verse 31. "For this reason a man will leave his father and mother and be united to his wife, and the two will become one flesh." Again, we see the attention God gives the husband, for he is to come out from under his parents' authority and now establish a union with his wife.

Two becoming one flesh seems like an obvious result when considering marriage and its consummation. However, there is more to discover than what we see on the surface. In view of the statement's inclusion in the same sentence that describes man's separating himself from his father and mother, it is apparent that we have a contrast to inspect. Before a man grows into adulthood, he has an obvious union as a child with his family. But even before that, he had a physical union with his mother. Hidden away in her womb, they shared blood, oxygen, nutrients, growing bodies and possibly some food aversions! There is a unique mother and child bond that begins long before the father sets his eyes upon the newborn. Is it any wonder that some women have a difficult time separating themselves from their little ones, even if that little one is 25 years old? I laugh when I think about a conversation I witnessed between two moms of adult children. The one who is distraught over her son is simply told by the other, "Cut the cord." In reality, the physical procedure had taken place nearly two decades prior to this conversation, but the necessary separation that would lead to maturity and confidence in his manhood was yet to come. It certainly would be unhealthy for this mother to enter into his future union with his wife, yet that is what can happen if God's Word is ignored.

Unfortunately, I know of messy marriages involving a man and his two women. Perhaps you find your husband seemingly more devoted to his mother than to you. God has made it clear in both the Old and the New Testaments that the husband must come out from that former parental authority in order to be united to his wife. At the same time, leaving his parents' authority does not make him a free agent. A husband may be head of his home, but Christ is the head of him. And ladies, we want that to be the case. It should help us at all times knowing God holds everyone accountable, including our husbands. A pastor once explained the submissive wife's role using the image of her bowed before her husband, only so the long arm of God can swing and hit her man directly when he needs it!

Christ is included in the Love Triangle as the One who bonds the two.

We now have arrived at the key to success in marriage: Christ is included in the Love Triangle as the One who bonds the two. What used to be a triangle of three between the son and his parents now consists of the husband, the wife and Christ. Jesus is the bonding agent for every married couple of faith. The two becoming one flesh is not only a physical act, but an emotional and spiritual act as well. In fact, hearing a dear friend describe a very difficult divorce that she experienced years earlier, she used words such as "tearing apart" and "ripping." Obviously, there is more to the uniting as husband and wife than a mere document with signatures and the state seal.

When a minister joins two in marriage, he finalizes the ceremony by saying, "What God has joined together, let no man put asunder" (Matthew 19:6). This means that what God creates is not to be destroyed by man. Yet, we see many selfish acts done by one or both spouses that completely wreck the home. Unfaithfulness in marriage is, in reality, a breaking of one's covenant with God. It destroys trust within the marriage and has the ability to affect future generations of family members. Marital unfaithfulness is the only exception Christ offers to the sin of adultery committed by those who divorce and marry again (Matthew 19:9). However, many couples that have dealt with adultery have chosen to forgive and found healing in their marriages through the restoration of God's love at work in and through them. However, preventing adultery is always the best option. Flee from all forms of sexual immorality and heed the Word of God found in Malachi 2:15- 16.

> *Has not the Lord made them one? In flesh and spirit they are His. And why one? Because He was seeking godly offspring. So guard yourself in your spirit, and do not break faith with the wife of your youth.*

> *"I hate divorce," says the Lord God of Israel, "and I hate a man's covering himself with violence as well as with his garment," says the Lord Almighty.*

Scripture clearly states that a spouse who chooses to leave based on his or her unwillingness to accept the faith of the other is free to go (1 Corinthians 7:15). In addition, those who are in danger of physical harm at the hands of an abuser should quickly separate themselves from that situation. Again, I have seen God still heal a marriage where one who once felt intimidated, later witnessed a changed heart and a changed husband. God deserves all of the glory for their restored marriage today.

There is no single example covering the spectrum of all marital experiences. It is always commendable to seek out godly counseling services. Many Christian counselors have been instrumental in God's plan to restore the broken-hearted in marriages.

Just as God emphatically declares that no man shall undo the union between a husband and wife, the enemy of our soul works fervently in direct opposition. Satan is intent on destruction of the home, and unfortunately, many cooperate with his plan simply because they are deceived. It is time to open our eyes to the truth as presented in Ephesians 6:12. It states, "For our struggle is not against flesh and blood, but against the rulers, against the authorities, against the powers of this dark world and against the spiritual forces of evil in the heavenly realms." Paul, the Apostle and writer of Ephesians, is inspired by the Holy Spirit to disclose the secret to successful and godly relationships. The revelation comes at the end of his discourse on marriages and other relationships. Husbands and wives can please the Father in heaven as they relate honorably to one another and choose to stand firm when tempted to stand in opposition to their spouse. How often do we fail to realize that it's not our spouse causing problems; it is actually the enemy baiting us to fight and destroy relationships?

What do we call our family members but "our flesh and blood?" God wants us to know that this struggle is not against them! It's against the spiritual forces of evil, and when they come knocking on the door of your home, you must "stand your ground, and after you have done everything...stand" (Eph. 6:13). God's work of salvation, His eternal Word and the Spirit's indwelling enable us to be thoroughly equipped to overcome every spiritual battle. It is only up to us to recognize the type of battle it is and to get engaged on that same level. We declare God's Word over our situations. The devil's lies hold no power over us when we stand on the Truth!

I can attest to times when I sensed that things were going to quickly escalate and spin out of control if I had caved to the verbal fight ensuing. I knew where to run for refuge, and I found my God to be faithful to grant me peace in His shadow. I have actually retreated to a solitary place simply to pray and rebuke Satan. I'm not sure how I learned this strategy. I can only surmise that in the little instruction in the things of God that I had as a child, it seemed to center on the truth of spiritual warfare. I knew that God is always victorious, and I only need to call upon the name of Jesus. I learned as a child that Satan is endlessly trying to lead God's children astray. My eyes are open to his ultimate plan of destruction. God warns us to "be self-controlled and alert. Your enemy the devil prowls around like a roaring lion looking for someone to devour" (1 Peter 5:8). My best advice to equip you for keeping watch is to especially be on guard during the times of disappointment. Satan is an opportunist and will attack when we are dealing with experiences such as loss, betrayal, sadness and confusion. He first targets our hearts with discouragement, which may seem rather harmless, but he aims to see it progress to despair. If he can cause us to think there is no hope in the situation, he is able to make great strides, because his next guided step down to the pit of hell is disillusionment. In this state, one will question if God even cares. Doubt arises concerning God's faithfulness. If Satan continues to infect our souls unnoticed, we will descend into a depression. Feeling abandoned and without purpose, one is more apt to question if there is any reason to continue living. Believe it or not, death is not even the end goal of the demonic descent. John 10:10 states, "The thief comes only to steal and kill and destroy," meaning there is yet a greater work beyond his scheme to kill. Satan aims to destroy, period. One life snuffed out is not sufficient because "Death and Destruction are never satisfied" (Prov. 27:20). To rid the earth of an influential life is to destroy the future ministry to countless souls! My heart cries out to all who will listen so that we may wake up to the scheme of the enemy. He is stealing from us the joy of our salvation and the privilege we share as co-heirs with Christ. This is not the plan of God! John 10:10 also states that Jesus came so we would have life to the full. We must know the Word of God! Knowing the truth ensures our quick detection of a lie!

It is time to take a stand for your marriage. You are not beyond hope. Tell the devil that his deception no longer has any power over your home. Start blessing your marriage with your mouth and believe that it will live and not die so that you can declare the wonders of the Lord (Psalm 118:17). The next time the opportunity arises to nag, complain or degrade the other, shut your mouth from its partnering with Satan. Choose instead to trust God to help you mend the broken walls. But this time around, make sure that Jesus Christ is the foundation to your fortress. Scripture declares that any effort to build upon a foundation other than Jesus is likened to building a house upon sand. When the storm rages and the waves rush in, the house built upon sand will fall. Oceanfront houses built on the sand and falling into the ocean is a sad reality at the beaches I often visit. In the Outer Banks of North Carolina, we have walked along the beach and under houses whose pilings are splashed with the incoming tide. We know that it is only a matter of time before one fatal hurricane or nor'easter will bring enough of a storm surge to wash that house out to sea. Let it not be so for our marriages. Jesus is the solid foundation for our homes. If this word reaches you right as you are convinced it's time to give up, take my advice and ask Him to come into your hearts, home and marriage. He is for you and for your family. He has all the power and wisdom to give you to keep your home intact.

One of my biggest revelations regarding Jesus being the glue that binds us together is based on the teaching of the fruit of the Spirit. The fruit that the Spirit of Christ produces in our lives is evident when we yield to His sovereignty. Galatians 5:22 discloses the multi-faceted fruit that is completely divine and not at all a by-product of our human nature. "But the fruit of the Spirit is love, joy, peace, patience, kindness, goodness, faithfulness, gentleness and self-control." Many of us honestly can say we experience moments of operating in some or all of these traits. However, even on our best days, we are completely limited in our natural strength to manifest the fruit of the Spirit. For example, love, in the original Greek language of the New Testament, is not the brotherly or romantic love that we might understand. The word "love" used in the scripture above is "agape," a self-sacrificing love.

This is the love that husbands are called to in serving their wives (Galatians 5:25).

A godly husband knows he is assigned headship by God and will perfectly fulfill his role by laying down his own life for his wife. No person relying upon human nature can operate in this state all the time. But for those who stay in step with the Spirit as He daily fills them and leads them, self-sacrificing love is a reality.

> The mind of sinful man is death, but the mind controlled by the Spirit is life and peace; the sinful mind is hostile to God. It does not submit to God's law, nor can it do so. Those controlled by the sinful nature cannot please God.
>
> You, however, are controlled not by the sinful nature but by the Spirit if the Spirit of God lives in you (Romans 8: 6-9).

I have learned that we should consider the nine components of the fruit of the Spirit as books on a shelf with love and self-control serving as the bookends. All of the other aspects of the fruit are found within the confines of these two. This is especially true in marriages where the working of the Holy Spirit produces love and self-control. We then find ourselves walking in obedience to God's command to love and submit.

> *The divine nature of Christ is produced in us and binds us. No other love has that same ability to sacrifice self.*

As with all godly character traits, we can expect to see an increase in self-control with each opportunity we practice it. Self-control literally affects every aspect of life, and I personally see its biggest impact in the ability to control the tongue. As a wife, I have a call to not only submit to my husband's authority, but to also respect him in the process. What harm might I cause if I simply go through the motions of submission while rebelling with my mouth in protest or getting in the last word? Much of the wisdom of Proverbs deals with the reality of ill-spoken words, but in particular, Proverbs 19:13 addresses the wife's speech: "a quarrelsome wife is like a constant dripping." Ouch. Have you been there before? I know I have. I have used words to hurt and even to subvert my husband's rule. A failure to submit to my husband is rebellion to God, "for the husband is the head of the wife…" (Eph. 5:23).

Let us open our eyes to these conditions and others that allow unrest into our marriages. Let us recognize the deceptive work of the enemy whose only goal is to reap destruction. In weakness we have fallen prey to his power of suggestion. We have believed that our significant other is the significant source of unhappiness in our lives. It is all a lie. What else can be expected from the father of lies (John 8:44)?

"God did not give us a spirit of timidity, but a spirit of power, of love and of self-discipline" (2 Timothy 1:7). To permit the Holy Spirit's guidance in our lives is to be perfectly equipped for successful marriages. We desperately need His supernatural power to flow in and through us. The divine nature of Christ is produced in us and binds us. No other love has that same ability to sacrifice self. No other means of self-discipline brings one to complete submission. It is by the Spirit alone that the two become one.

Study Questions for Chapter Five

1. What counsel would you offer to the married person who has yet to come out from under parental authority?

2. What evidence of Christ's uniting the two to become one is seen in your marriage?

3. What is Satan's path to destruction of the marriage? Have you ever found yourself deceived and descending along that path?

4. With what weapons do we have to fight when engaged in spiritual warfare?

5. Are you currently facing a disappointment in your marriage? Have you prayed for your spouse and for God's direction to resolve the issue?

6. Consider the following scenario: a married couple has a serious discussion concerning a disagreement over the sharing of responsibilities around the home. What would be the outcome if both aim to stay in step with the Spirit?

GREG AND TRACEY

Greg and Tracey enjoyed several years together in their marriage before starting a family. But by the time Tracey was pregnant with their second child, they both noticed that their relationship had changed. She was concerned and noticed that Greg had become increasingly withdrawn from the family. Shortly after the baby was born, she asked him if everything was ok. Upon being asked a second time, Greg revealed that he did not wish to remain married because he was unsure if this was the life he wanted.

Greg's announcement shocked Tracey because with all of her focus on their children, she had been oblivious to what had been happening between them.

She now realizes that Greg had needed attention, but she had neglected him since becoming a mother. Tracey had permitted her focus to shift entirely from him to their children.

They spent the next six months of their life merely existing. They made a few attempts to go out on dates and rekindle the romance between them. In all of her wondering if the plan was effective, Tracey typically realized by the time they got home that it was not changing the situation.

> **Tracey knew that it was going to be God alone who would change Greg's heart.**

They continued to live together and go to church together. Each Sunday, she dropped the girls off in the nursery and preschool class and walked alone to their adult class praying that God would speak to Greg. She asked God to help Greg see that he would want to remain a part of their lives.

Tracey continually sought the Lord during this most difficult trial of her life. She relied heavily upon Him and knew that He would speak to her each time she opened the Word of God. Even when Greg announced that he found a place to live and would move out in a few days, she still experienced God's amazing peace. There were times when the peace came and went, but she prayed and cried out to God through it all. She grew in her devotion to the Lord because He was her only source of comfort from the deep pain of rejection.

Only a few friends knew about the condition of their marriage. A couple of them sought the Lord on their behalf by fasting and praying for them. Tracey knew that it was going to be God alone who would change Greg's heart.

The day before Greg planned to move out, they went to church together as a family. Again, Tracey dropped the girls off, made her way to the adult class, and silently prayed for God to speak to Greg. Right then she heard the Holy Spirit say, "You have been praying the wrong thing. God is always speaking; pray that Greg will hear."

Later that day, Greg called her to say that he would be home in ten minutes. This was strange due to the fact that his phone calls home had stopped long ago. When he arrived, he shared that something was different. He felt like God was talking to him in Sunday school earlier that day. He also said that he wanted their marriage to work and he was committed to staying together.

From that day forward, their marriage changed and continued to flourish. No longer was there the struggle of giving up on the relationship. Tracey is thankful for the trial because it taught her to trust God completely. They both learned that walking with the Lord and keeping their lives centered on Him was the only way to have a successful marriage.

Chapter Six

THE
SANCTUARY

Through the process of dissection of Ephesians 5:22- 33, we have looked at the role of each major player described in the passage. The concluding statement of the sermon wraps up Paul's message with, "...each of you also must love his wife as he does himself, and the wife must respect her husband." We have come full circle. We have looked carefully into the heart of God to understand His design for marriage. It is appropriate now to bring it all together. In the end, wives need to know that they are loved and protected, and husbands need respect in the home.

Both of these ideals are reality when we decide to follow God's Word concerning marriages.

The Love Triangle consists of the husband, his wife, and Jesus. Christ is the One who binds them in covenant love with one another and with the Father in heaven. A marriage built according to God's design is a one that brings Him glory. Therefore, a God-honoring marriage is a form of worship. The places where we worship vary, but we can always define the homes of such marriages as sanctuaries.

Viewing the home as a sanctuary is a concept that I have often revisited in our more than twenty years of marriage. The realization of it hits me freshly whenever we are faced with uncontrollable chaos in life. There have been times of great discouragement concerning the lives of our loved ones, and we find ourselves saddened by their circumstances. Jon and I will cry and pray as we intercede on their behalf, then quickly respond with thanksgiving to God for the abiding peace in our home.

> **What do we do to protect ourselves from life's uncertainties and acts of evil? We run to the Deliverer.**

The changing world in which we live is commonly noted as being in a state of chaos. The daily news reports of economic instability, national uprisings, nuclear warheads in the hands of dictators, and devastating results of acts of nature are just a few of the issues that can strike a man's heart with fear. Think about the day America stopped breathing momentarily to soak in the realization that we had suffered an attack on our soil. On September 11, 2001, an airplane crashed in a field and others were flown into buildings, killing thousands in an instant. What do we do to protect ourselves from life's uncertainties and acts of evil? We run to the Deliverer. Psalm 91:1 states, "He who dwells in the shelter of the Most High will rest in the shadow of the Almighty." For those of us who have built a home upon the foundation of Jesus Christ, we don't have to run far. The peace of God within us will affect the atmosphere wherever we are, but we can be certain that security is experienced within the walls of our homes.

Concerning a young child's understanding of 9/11, my friend told me that in the days following the tragedy, her 2-year old son was able to state that he was not afraid because he knew God was with him. It was amazing to me that while many people in our nation were shaken to the core, this little child of God could declare with certainty that he was safe in the Father's care. He experienced the effect of his home as a sanctuary. While chaos reigned on the outside, he was able to dwell in a place of safety and peace.

Exactly two years later, our area in Virginia was preparing for a category 5- hurricane to make landfall. Its strength fluctuated for a few days while it moved through the Atlantic. Still, the day before the storm was an unsettling one as meteorologists tried to predict the path of the weakening system. Residents made all of the necessary arrangements in the form of evacuations or gathering of supplies should all utilities be lost. I remember standing in my dining room and looking out the window while I prayed. I told the Lord that I had no idea what the next day would bring. There was pending damage and loss with a storm this size, but we did not know how close to home it would come. In my heart, I knew that strong winds or a tornado spin-off could wipe out a house in an instant. It was at that moment that I had to entrust my life to Him and believe that even if property or life was destroyed, it was the soul that really mattered.

The winds howled like crazy that night. Our family chose to sleep in a room located farthest away from trees that could possibly fall into the house. Personally, I had a good night's sleep and enjoyed the rest I found in the Lord. The next day, we awoke to the reality of widespread destruction. Flooding wreaked havoc in the low-lying areas and fallen tress destroyed property everywhere. The city schools were closed for weeks while streets were cleared and power lines were restored. Over three billion dollars worth of damage assessed in the storm's aftermath confirmed that chaos had visited us.

Figuratively speaking, we cannot necessarily control the storms that affect our lives. We can, however, change the atmosphere surrounding us by choosing to place our full trust in God alone. That is the reality of the sanctuary. It remains a safe haven in spite of the tempest's threats.

One of my greatest pleasures as a homemaker is cultivating a sanctuary experience for my family. All homemakers truly value a sense of serenity and desire the family's enjoyment of the same. I am not saying that we manufacture peace; it is impossible to do. The real peace of God comes from knowing one's right standing with Him and trusting Him in everything. In essence, we cultivate a peaceful environment when we take time to nurture the spirit. Each family member should individually pursue the building of his or her relationship with the Father. Listen to Jesus' invitation to any in need of peace: "Come to Me, all you who are weary and burdened, and I will give you rest. Take my yoke upon you and learn from Me, for I am gentle and humble in heart, and you will find rest for your souls. For my yoke is easy and my burden is light" (Matthew 11:28-30). We get to accept Christ's offer every day. He genuinely offers His rest in exchange for the heaviness of life's circumstances. It almost sounds too good to be true. To really know the Lord is to trust Him. Perhaps you are ready to trust Him right now with something that is weighing on you. Cast that burden to Him. He is the Prince of Peace.

If you were to measure the sanctuary effect in your home, what hindrances might you discover? Is there a lack of peace due to on-going arguments? If so, talk about your desire to take action in obedience to God's instruction. If you both seek to fulfill your roles as a submissive wife and a self-sacrificing husband, fighting will cease.

Recently, I have been hearing more about the health of the family, and specialists are in agreement that children suffer when there is strife in the home. "In fact, children are barometers of family tension, registering parental fears and rage and sadness better than the best meteorological instruments register the weather," states psychologist Dr. Benjamin Garber. 1 For this reason, we must be on guard against the stresses of life. The more we ignore a trust in God, the more we will allow stresses to disrupt the peace that God intends for our homes and lives.

To say that fighting needs to be eliminated in order to bring peace to the home is to merely prescribe a band-aid remedy for an issue with a deeper source. Money, children and sex are just a few of the common causes of arguments in marriages. For solution, we must look to the Word of God for His truth and guidance on each of these and other issues causing unrest. Husbands and wives need to talk about the issues that are not in alignment with Scripture. We then humble ourselves before God and one another and confess our sin of rebellion. We re-prioritize our goals in marriage and choose to live in unity with our spouses and with the Lord.

Husbands and wives, it is our responsibility to set the tone. Either our families are experiencing a sanctuary home life, or they are aware that at any moment, chaos will reign. Make the decision. "Choose this day whom you will serve." Then declare as Joshua did, "As for me and my house, we will serve the Lord" (Joshua 24:15).

Study Questions for Chapter Six

1. Based on Ephesians 5:33, what is the core need of the wife? Of the husband?

2. What prescription do you seek when faced with the uncontrollable chaos of life?

3. What would it take to experience peace in your home even in the midst of a storm?

4. How are children affected by stress in the home? Who bears the authority to create a sanctuary environment?

Chapter Seven

COME AWAY, MY LOVER

Of course a book on marriage is going to delve into the topic of intimacy. The Ephesians passage establishes the foundational truth upon which we can now build healthy intimacy within the marriage. There are so many issues that affect our relational health, and if they go unresolved, intimacy or the lack of it, will only complicate the situation. We will seek truth in God's Word concerning the sexual relationship between a husband and a wife. Do not be shocked to learn that He has much to say about it! After all, God is the Creator of marriage, and he formed us to enjoy one another on all levels: mentally, relationally, emotionally and physically.

Sex is given as a gift to a husband and wife, and when experienced within the confines of marriage, it is a wonderful source of growth for the couple.

1 Corinthians 7:2–5 emphasizes that a husband and wife are to fulfill one another's needs. God desires us to understand that the wife's body does not belong to herself alone but also to her husband. Likewise, the husband's body belongs to his wife as well as to himself. And so, we are instructed to "not deprive each other except by mutual consent and for a time." Paul, the author of 1 Corinthians, also states that this mutually agreed upon time of refraining from sexual intimacy is for the devoting of oneself to prayer. Finally, we are advised to come back together again so that temptation to sin sexually does not overcome us due to a lack of self-control.

Paul, inspired by the Holy Spirit, stresses the importance of sexual purity. The temptation for sexual sin is still very strong and just as easy to fall prey to in our generation as it was for the Corinthian believers. Paul poses the question, "Do you not know that your bodies are members of Christ Himself? Shall I then take the members of Christ and unite them with a prostitute? Never! Do you not know that he who unites himself with a prostitute is one with her in body? For it is said, 'The two will become one flesh'" (1 Cor. 6: 15-16).

Repeatedly, Paul warns the unrepentant, sexually immoral that they will have no share in the inheritance of the kingdom of God. So, according to the Scripture, if there are intimacy issues in the marriage, there is also greater temptation for sexual sin and consequences of possibly eternal significance for those who fall into sin.

> ***Romance requires an investment of time and creativity that perhaps was abandoned once the courtship ended.***

Romance requires an investment of time and creativity that perhaps was abandoned once the courtship ended. Recently, a friend commented that her boyfriend treated her to a wonderful day at the spa. She was talking about the man that she had been married to for decades, but I love that she called him her boyfriend. It is evident that romance is alive in that marriage. It cost him to send his wife off to receive royal treatment, but he is acknowledging her as the princess that she is. Women love to be valued like that.

And what do men like? I do fear oversimplifying a response, but men are easily stimulated by sight. It can be very difficult for a woman to understand that her husband does not require the same mental and emotional investment to be primed for sexual intimacy. Yet, if he is taught that his wife needs and values time with him that is in addition to their intimate moments, he will act upon the reward of enjoying a greater connection.

Husbands and wives need to prioritize their relationship and at times make some sacrifices to focus solely on their togetherness. Some couples have a weekly date night, and they work hard to prevent other things from causing conflict with their designated time for one another.

I'm personally a fan of heading out of town with my beloved. This has not always been easy for us to do. But with the help of family and friends to watch the children, we have taken romantic escapes and have memories that will last a lifetime.

If you take a look at the Song of Solomon, it is evident that God Himself is the Creator of the romantic escape. The Sunday school teacher of our young married couples said he would not teach from that steamy book in the Bible! He suggested that we couples get alone in our bedrooms and read the material for ourselves! Solomon's poem enlightens our understanding of God's love for His bride, the Church. Recall that God uses the uniting of husband and wife to illustrate the intimate relationship between Christ and the Church (Eph. 5:32). Nothing else in our physical existence can come any closer to depicting the sweet fellowship between the Lord and the Church than the relationship between a husband and a wife.

In the beautifully written lines of Solomon's Song of Songs, we find romantically scripted words of physical beauty and attraction. We find desire and enjoyment of sexual pleasure. And to further stress my point on the importance of the get-away, we read the words, "Come away, my lover…." Just a few lines remain beyond those words, but in following the example of my former teacher, you should probably grab the Word of God and finish reading at your convenience.

Recognizing where we are in today's culture of sexual freedom, it is imperative to look at the baggage in marriages resulting from past sexual encounters. It is the rare couple that enters into the marriage covenant with their virginity in tact. To combat this issue, the church is called by God to illuminate His Word concerning sexual intimacy so that the young generation can indeed remain pure. In our church family, we are taking every opportunity to speak truthfully with our young people. Older generations may be shocked at how forthright pastors have to be on the topic of sex. But in a world where the message of sexual perversion and immorality are loudly announced as the new norm, the church must be vigilant to instruct the young with truth. The most biblical approach given is the example of Joseph who foreknew his response to a proposal to engage in an act of sexual immorality. He said, "How can I do such a wicked thing and sin against God?" (Genesis 39:9). We see that Joseph's reaction to Potiphar's wife was not based on fear of being caught by the seductress' husband and his master. He was aware that God's eyes are always upon his children, and an act of adultery would never be hidden from Him.

Be sure to teach the young people in your life this level of integrity. Also teach them to avoid situations where they will be more readily tempted to compromise their goal to remain pure. We must understand, however, that most young people are not making a pledge of sexual purity. Unless we adults educate them and counsel them in the truth of God's Word, they see no need to enter into a future marriage as virgins. The world simply does not promote the message of purity.

I understand from years of teaching young people that sexual temptation is a huge part of their lives. Not only do they face peer pressure and sexual messages in all forms of media, but they also have the hormonal surges awakening desires within them. The missing link of understanding is that God forbids their sexual intimacy not to be cruel and keep them from having fun. He has preserved it for marriage alone. It is His design to protect us and promote healthy lives. The gift of sex for the married is intended as the most heightened level of knowing one's spouse through the mutual enjoyment of one another. It builds an intimacy between two that is only healthy to have if they plan to remain together with no other outsiders privy to the same level of connection.

This is so contrary to the way the world looks at the meaning of sex. They believe that a night together is just that. In their deceived thinking, they have "moved on" the day after. However, at some point in time, the sexually promiscuous will experience negative effects from every instance where a lack of self-control was demonstrated. Consequences will have to be dealt with. Ideally, one will experience godly sorrow that in turn leads to genuine repentance. This is the action required of all of us who have turned away from God. We seek forgiveness and confess a desire to never fall back into the former habit of sin.

Entering into marriage with a history of sexual activity necessitates a time of open communication and healing. All previous physical and/or emotional connections require a spiritual severance through prayerful repentance. Each union needs to be named and repented of so that it may not have any further impact upon the lives of the married couple. Think of it the way we delete files from our computer hard drives. We highlight the unwanted file then hit the delete button. The same must happen with all former relationships in order for the marriage to have an optimal level of healthy intimacy. It is as simple as praying, "God, I sever all physical, emotional and spiritual ties that I had with _____. I will no longer allow any influence of that previous relationship to affect my relationship with You and others. Please forgive me for stepping out of Your will in creating a bond that was not holy, and give me the resolve to not fall again into sin."

If revealing past mistakes is viewed as an embarrassing and debasing activity, be advised that the Father in heaven already knows every deed done under the cover of darkness. Also, being open and honest with your spouse is the ideal foundation to build upon, even if it includes revealing dirty laundry. Deal with it now before it deals you a difficult hand in the future. In addition, the deception of the enemy is broken when we allow God's light to dispel the past darkness in our hearts. Satan's stronghold remains over us when we are shamed into secrecy. Revealing truth completely wrecks his deceptive power, and we are set free.

God desires every married couple to enjoy their intimacy with no shame. Ideally, this naturally will occur as the couple enters into their marriage in purity. If that is not the case, they will clear the air with confession and repentance prior to marriage. At the same time, the message of healthy intimacy is also for those who have already been married for years. God is able and willing to restore the broken places in your life. His name is Redeemer, and He will take your mistakes of the past and work them into something beautiful. It is never too late to make things right in your marriage. Forgiveness and healing are possible through the love and power of God. If it is your desire to build a fresh foundation of honesty in your marriage, you can start today. God will be your strength and your shelter. Look ahead with confidence to the days when you will say to your beloved with a clear conscious, "Come away, my lover."

Study Questions for Chapter Seven

1. In what ways does our society honor and promote sexual purity?

2. Do you and your spouse experience times of refraining from sexual intimacy? If so, do you believe the purpose is God-honoring?

3. Lack of sexual intimacy is a marriage-killer. How might Satan lead a couple into a state devoid of intimacy?

4. What evidence is there in your marriage to prove that romance is alive? If there is none, are you willing to initiate it?

5. A history of hidden sexual sin needs to be confessed and dealt with. If you or your spouse has past mistakes, what steps have you taken to seek restoration? If no action has occurred, what do you need to do today to build healthy intimacy in your marriage?

Chapter Eight

CHOOSE THE
BETTER WAY

This final message to married couples aims to strengthen our daily relationships. If there is one thing to say in culmination of all of the other topics, this point is it. In any situation where we are given a choice in how to respond, God wants us to know that there is a better way. If there is a better way, then it is safe to say that there is a worse way. If you are like me, you want to have the wisdom necessary to always choose the way that pleases the Father and eliminates regrets.

Mary and Martha have invited Jesus and His disciples to their home as recorded in Luke 10:38-42. Mary sits at Jesus' feet as he teaches while Martha busily makes preparations for the meal. The hard-working sister becomes indignant with her apparently lazy sibling and asks Jesus to correct Mary for not pitching in to help. The Lord's response is tender: "Martha, Martha…you are worried and upset about many things, but only one thing is needed. Mary has chosen what is better, and it will not be taken away from her."

This familiar account of two sisters may not seem to fit the topic of marriage. Yet, the two responses, the better one and the worse one, we will consider in light of our daily choices affecting marriage.

Mary's sitting at the Master's feet represents a humble stance. She is in essence stating that there is more to learn, and she knows that she can position herself to gain by simply sitting and listening. On the other hand, Martha's flurry of activity represents a prideful stance. It is obvious that she believes her work and responsibilities are far too important to simply be still and know that Jesus is Lord. Rather than try to identify ourselves with one or the other sister, I want us to realize that in any given situation, we can respond with either a humble or prideful heart. The goal is to always choose the way of humility. This exemplifies the character of Christ and prevents unnecessary heartache, because "When pride comes, then comes disgrace, but with humility comes wisdom" (Proverbs 11:2).

> *The result of pride is strife, but if we desire rest or peace, we must learn it from the Prince of Peace.*

In our natural strength, pride will be at the base of all of our thoughts, beliefs and interactions in our marriages. It will rear its ugly head at every given opportunity. Only those who have been taught Jesus' ways and daily follow the Spirit's leading will keep their flesh instinct bridled. Remember, Jesus offers to teach us humility that, in turn, leads to rest for our souls. He says, "learn from Me, for I am gentle and humble in heart... "(Matthew 11:29). We have to learn how to have peace because our prideful nature will not produce it. The result of pride is strife, but if we desire rest or peace, we must learn it from the Prince of Peace. Gentleness and humility are natural to Christ because they are inherent to His divine nature.

The best way to illustrate this truth is to explore some typical challenges that married couples face. Let us begin with the topic of money. I have concern for those who have a "her money and his money" policy. It gives the appearance of selfishness, the ruling motive of the worldly. For example, those who are very wealthy often enter marriage with a prenuptial agreement because their money is theirs, and the spouse is not going to get his or her hands on it should they divorce. That is the way of the world.

Christ–followers marry with the belief that they will never separate, so their money should not be handled separately. Even the first followers of Jesus stayed together and had everything in common. Those were brothers and sisters in Christ who shared their wealth with one another and those in need. We should increase the expectation of husbands and wives to share their wealth with one another. If you are currently keeping separate accounts, ask yourselves what purpose that serves. Are there trust issues? If keeping separate accounts is viewed as the way to resolve them, it is inadequate. Lack of trust will reap destruction in other areas in the marriage. Deal with the lack of trust in general, and begin to jointly handle the finances.

Some feel that they can better hide their erratic spending if financial accounts are kept separate. This is another issue that affects other aspects of the marriage. The heart that justifies hiding the truth about spending will be tempted to do the same in other issues the couple faces. Come clean and get some accountability arranged with your spouse.

We cannot assume that it is always the wife who has a lack of self-control when it comes to money. Some men are also spendthrifts, and the Lord has brought balance into their lives in the form of a wife. Therefore, help one another to live within your means while keeping your finances out in the open.

The stance of the prideful declares, "My money is my money and is off limits!" Lay this incorrect belief down if you are a child of God. Know that the earth is the Lord's along with everything in it, so to lay claim to any amount of money is in direct contradiction to the Word of God. We have been called to be faithful stewards of all that God has entrusted to us.

The humble spouse understands that if even his or her body is not theirs alone (1 Cor. 7:4), then surely that contained in a wallet on their body is not theirs alone. The humble always trust God in the surrendering of their autonomy. His plans for the married couple are rich if they look to Him in all things.

Money is a popular topic with God. More than 800 scriptures address the topic. For many, it is the ultimate litmus test of complete trust in Him. Are you willing to surrender your finances? Wives, we are called to submit to our husbands as to the Lord. Do you believe that you can trust God with financial decisions? Then trust your husbands. Men, do you truly desire to follow God's marriage design and die to self as Christ died for the Church? Then be prepared to sacrifice financially.

You joined in marriage with the intention to share life together. Do not allow the topic of money to divide you in your relationship. Rather, humble yourselves and jointly consider your household's budget. If there is a lack of control with spending, seek financial counseling and create a plan to get back on the right track. There are effective tools created by Christian advisors to help us manage our finances. The first step is to humbly acknowledge that we need help.

An Internet search of Christian Finance Solutions will connect you to a variety of resources available. You may want to also seek out local churches offering personal finance courses. The investment of time and money in a class and/or materials will be worth the expenditure.

Another hot commodity in marriage that will challenge us in our pursuit to be humble is the designation of our time. Time is actually more costly than any other asset; it can never be replaced or regained. There is one thing that I have learned when it comes to choosing humility in the sacrificing of my time: if I freely give my time as the Spirit leads me to give, I will be rewarded with the joy of obedience and the time to do all of the things that I thought would not get done otherwise. There will be countless times in marriages where husbands and wives will have opportunity to humbly fulfill their roles by sacrificing their time. Wives will submit to their husbands by humbly taking the time to do what he needs her to do. I realize this is so much easier to write than to actually do. The prideful nature within says, "I don't want to take the time to do what you ask me to do. What I am focused on doing is far more important." At least that is what Martha may have said. Look though at Mary, in humble submission, taking the necessary time to do what is pleasing to the Master.

What challenges lie ahead for us to be humble spouses in all situations we face in marriage! We will find ourselves battling the prideful nature within as we deal with household responsibilities, disagreements, work schedules, friends, children, and the list goes on. Because the humble approach is not the operating mode of the flesh, we must learn it from the Master. We have to be intentional to be successful in marriage. It is going to require blood (Jesus' was sufficient), sweat (our daily battles against the forces of evil and our own selfish desires) and tears (these come in our prayers of surrender). God is for you, Child of His. He gives you today to make a fresh start if you desire. God also gives us the opportunity to improve and strengthen our relationships. Marriage is meant to last, but if left up to only two, that may not be the outcome. Choose three. The Love Triangle endures all things.

Study Questions for Chapter Eight

1. Give an example of strife produced in your marriage as a result of your acting in pride.

2. In what area have you already been made aware of your need to learn humility from Christ?

3. Do you recognize an area of weakness in your marriage due to the prideful stance of you or your spouse? How might the humility of Christ turn that situation around?

4. What philosophy do you and your spouse share on personal finance? Do you see a need for improvement in the handling of your personal finances? Are you willing to seek out Godly counsel?

5. Memorize Matthew 11: 28-30.

6. Can you name all the ways that Christ binds the husband and wife in covenant love?

A Prayer for Marriages

Father in heaven, Your Name is glorified. Your life is given to me in Christ Jesus the Lord. In You, I have the power to rise above every circumstance and force that opposes me. I will not fear the trial in my marriage, because Your Word states that You will never leave me or forsake me, nor will you give me a greater burden than I can bear. Today I commit to You my marriage, for it is You who joined us together with the ability to sustain us in Your love. Change my heart today to be free from past misconceptions and failures. I come under Your truth of who I am in Christ.

No weapon formed against me will prosper, because I am aware of the enemy's scheme to destroy that which You created. Today I put on the full armor of God so that I am ready to battle every lie and tactic of Satan. I believe that Your truth defeats every attempt at deception, and I sever any cooperation I had with the enemy's lies before today. Forgive me for my sins. Because I am Your child, I say with confidence, "The old has gone, the new has come."

I pray for my heart's renewal as I fill it with the truth of Your eternal Word. Purify my heart and renew a steadfast spirit within me. I believe You for a transformed life as I renew my mind, therefore escaping the patterns of this world. I desire to be able to test and approve your good, pleasing and perfect will for my life and my household.

I declare today that I will follow Your design for marriage as You clearly explain it in the Bible. I recognize and honor that the husband is the head of the wife. I understand that the husband is responsible for the wife as Christ is responsible for the church. I pray to hear the Spirit's leading daily as we operate in this paradigm.

I believe that the wife is the cherished treasure and will respect the husband's authority in the act of submission.

Today I partner with Christ to complete the union that I have with my spouse. I rely on Your Spirit, Jesus, to fill me afresh every day so that Your divine nature is at work in and through me. Because I have been given fullness in Christ, let the fruit of the Spirit be evident in my life in the form of love, joy, peace, patience, kindness, goodness, faithfulness, gentleness and self-control.

Today I choose to humble myself in seeking how I can better serve my spouse. As I follow Your Word, restore all the broken areas that resulted from my previous actions birthed in pride. Starting now, I choose the better way in attempting to consider my spouse better than myself.

And lastly, I rely on You, Eternal Father, to fashion a marriage built upon the foundation of Jesus Christ, the Lord. More than riches, this is the heritage that I want to hand down: a God-honoring marriage and a household that serves the Lord.

In Jesus' mighty name, Amen.

NOTES

Chapter One

Marriage Models

Daniel 1: 8 -20

William Strauss and Neil Howe, *Generations, The History of America's Future* (New York, NY: William Morrow and Co., Inc., 1991), 14.

US Census Bureau http://www.census.gov Table 1335, Marriage and Divorce Rates by Country: 1980-2008 (accessed September 19, 2011).

Chapter Two
A Glance Back

Jeremiah 29:13

Chapter Three
The Beauty of Submission

1.   Doug McIntosh, *Community Bible Study Commentary* (Colorado Springs, CO, 2008)

Chapter Four
Sacrificial Love

1 Peter 3:7

Chapter Six
The Sanctuary

Benjamin Garber, Ph.D., ADHD or not ADHD: Custody and Visitation Considerations, *New Hampshire Bar News*, New Hampshire Bar Association (Concord, NH, 2001)

About the Author

Renee Beamer is a passionate teacher of God's Word with a desire to see others experiencing fullness in Christ. She is wife to Jonathon, mother of Jacob and Jordan, and founder of Sharing Love and Truth Ministry. Her celebration of God's goodness is evident in her outreach to individuals, churches, communities and those abroad. Jon and Renee put their faith into action in the Dominican Republic through financial support of missions and education, church building, community outreach and media promotion. It is their joy to partner with Mitch and Debbie Martinez, full-time missionaries in La Vega, in seeing even more lives restored through the love of Christ Jesus. Proceeds from book sales continue to support this desperately needed ministry. To learn more, visit www.dominicanmissions. com.

Renee can be reached at:

Sharing Love and Truth
111 Overlook Cove, Newport News, VA 23602
Tel: (757.241.3131)
Web sites:
sharingloveandtruth.org
Twitter.com/ReneeBeamer
Facebook.com/ReneeBeamer